The War of 1812

by Lucia Raatma

Content Adviser: Richard J. Bell,
History Department,
Harvard University

Reading Adviser: Susan Kesselring, M.A., Literacy Educator,
Rosemount-Apple Valley-Eagan (Minnesota) School District

COMPASS POINT BOOKS
MINNEAPOLIS, MINNESOTA

Compass Point Books
3109 West 50th Street, #115
Minneapolis, MN 55410

Visit Compass Point Books on the Internet at *www.compasspointbooks.com*
or e-mail your request to *custserv@compasspointbooks.com*

On the cover: The U.S. ship *Constitution* (left) defeated the British ship *Guerriere*
on August 12, 1812.

Creative Director: Terri Foley
Managing Editor: Catherine Neitge
Editor: Nadia Higgins
Photo Researcher: Svetlana Zhurkina
Designer/Page production: Bradfordesign, Inc./Les Tranby
Cartographer: XNR Productions, Inc.
Educational Consultant: Diane Smolinski

Library of Congress Cataloging-in-Publication Data
Raatma, Lucia.
    The War of 1812 / by Lucia Raatma.
        p. cm. — (We the people)
Includes bibliographical references and index.
ISBN 0-7565-0848-7 (hardcover)
1. United States—History—War of 1812—Juvenile literature. I. Title. II.
We the people (Series) (Compass Point Books)
    E354.R33 2004
    973.5'2—dc22   2004016305

TABLE OF CONTENTS

ANOTHER WAR AGAINST GREAT BRITAIN

No doubt, you have heard of the Revolutionary War. Beginning in 1775, the American colonies fought for their freedom from Great Britain. When a peace treaty was finally signed in 1783, the United States of America was born. However, you may not know very much about the War of 1812. This was another conflict between the United States and Great Britain.

As the first president of the United States, George Washington had warned Americans to stay out of disagreements between foreign countries. Now, less than 30 years after the American Revolution had ended, staying out of a war between France and England seemed impossible.

In the early 1800s, France had a new leader, Napoleon Bonaparte, who was eager for power and wealth. He wanted to control all of Europe, and especially England, which had been at war with France for many years. One way to do this was to destroy England's sea trade. So Napoleon issued laws trying to shut off all trade between England and other countries. In turn, England tried to hurt French trade by declaring a blockade of all ports controlled by France.

French leader Napoleon Bonaparte waged a war against England that the United States wanted to avoid.

The young American nation enjoyed making money by trading goods with both countries and wanted to stay out of the conflict. However, England and France did not let that happen. Their shipping blockades had a terrible effect on American trade.

Great Britain said that U.S. ships wanting to trade with France had to stop at British ports to pay fees. At the same time, France ordered U.S. ships *not* to stop at British ports. The United States was angry about being put in such a difficult position.

5

The United States relied heavily on trade ships such as this one to carry goods to France and England.

However, the United States had more cause to be upset with England. British military ships had recently begun an unfair practice called impressment. They would capture U.S. trade ships and force U.S. sailors to work on British ships.

6

American sailors were forced into service with the British navy.
This practice, called impressment, outraged the American people.

The British said they were just taking back sailors who had
deserted, or illegally left, the British navy to work on
American ships. However, this was not always the case.
Often, American-born sailors were captured by the British.

7

The attack by the British ship Leopard *on the USS* Chesapeake *(right) almost started a war in 1807.*

In June 1807, the British ship *Leopard* stopped the USS *Chesapeake* in American waters. The British wanted to search for sailors who had left their navy. When the American captain did not let them onboard, the *Leopard* fired on the *Chesapeake*. Then British sailors captured four of the American crew and hanged one of them. Anger between the Americans and the British grew so strong that many feared war would break out.

8

In December 1807, President Thomas Jefferson tried to peacefully solve at least part of the problem. He supported a law, called the Embargo Act, to stop all trade between the United States and foreign countries. He thought this embargo would show England and France just how much they relied on trade with the United States. He hoped it would force the British and

President Thomas Jefferson worked to prevent the War of 1812.

French to work out a solution with the U.S. government.

This strategy did not work. The embargo was hard on the Americans. Ship owners in New England lost money, and sailors lost their jobs. Business people could not sell their goods to foreign countries, and Southern plantation owners could not sell their tobacco, cotton, and other crops

This cartoon makes fun of the Embargo Act by calling it "this cursed Ograbme."

overseas. The people of the United States were so frustrated with the Embargo Act that they nicknamed it the "Ograbme" act, which is *embargo* spelled backward.

10

THE DECISION TO ATTACK

Finally in 1810, Congress removed all restrictions on trade. However, it went on to say that the United States would trade only with the country that would give up its blockade. So if England relaxed its laws, the United States would not trade with France. If France relaxed its laws, the United States would not trade with England.

It was then that Napoleon saw his chance. He pretended to cooperate with the United States. So the United States stopped all trade to England once again. In the coming months, the Americans tried to work out a deal with England, too, but without success. The situation with England grew more and more frustrating.

By this time, James Madison was president of the United States. President Madison was cautious about entering a war, but many Americans supported the idea. Generally, people from the South and the West

James Madison became president in 1809.

wanted to go to war against England. Among them were Henry Clay of Kentucky, John C. Calhoun of South Carolina, and Andrew Jackson of Tennessee. Known as War Hawks, they wanted to show England that the United States was a strong nation. They also saw war as a way to gain more land. Settlers moving west were trying to take land from the American Indians, and the War Hawks saw the British as an obstacle to this effort. The British had sided with the Native Americans and even started giving them guns to defend themselves. Although today Americans have realized that it was unfair to take Native American

12

In 1811, Indians fought American troops at the Battle of Tippecanoe near present-day Lafayette, Indiana. Later, British weapons were found at the site, proving that the British were helping the Indians.

land, in the early 1800s, fairness was not considered. The government wanted the nation to grow. So the War Hawks wanted to get back at the British for helping the Native Americans.

13

In the meantime, those from the New England states wanted to avoid war. They depended on the sea trade, and England had a lot of power on the seas. They also were sympathetic to England and did not approve of the way Napoleon had been treating both England and the United States.

In the end, the War Hawks convinced President Madison that war was the only answer. They told him that America's pride was at stake. So in November 1811, Madison asked Congress to prepare the country for war. The members of Congress debated intensely for many months before finally declaring war on Great Britain on June 18, 1812.

John C. Calhoun

Andrew Jackson

Henry Clay

These three men, known as War Hawks, pushed for war against Great Britain.

15

BATTLES OF 1812

One may wonder how the United States could have made such a decision. In 1812, Great Britain was a far stronger nation. The United States had little money and a small army, with few trained officers. Because the U.S. Navy was so small, it had to hire private citizens with armed ships, called privateers, to fight. On top of that, New England—which was the richest part of the country—refused to help at all, withholding money and soldiers from the effort.

It was a good thing for the Americans that the British military was still occupied by a war with France. The British could not devote all their powerful forces to this new, less important fight. The end result was a war that was not an all-out struggle for either side. It was not often clear which side was winning the War of 1812, as each had its share of losses and victories in battle.

16

The Americans were full of confidence when they entered their battles in July 1812. They thought they could easily take Canadian land away from England, so they invaded Canada in areas between Montreal and Detroit, Michigan.

This map shows the major battles of the War of 1812.

17

American General William Hull (far right) surrenders to the British at Detroit in August 1812. The Indian chief Tecumseh (far left) was a British ally.

However, that early confidence was soon weakened. A British general named Isaac Brock joined forces with a Native American chief named Tecumseh. They captured Detroit, easily defeating General William Hull and his American soldiers in August 1812.

18

Other early battles in Canada were also unsuccessful for the U.S. troops. An American force lost the Battle of Queenston Heights in October when New York militia soldiers refused to cross the U.S.-Canada border. The backup soldiers were technically not allowed to leave the state. The following month, Americans marched to Lake Champlain but then retreated. Again, militia soldiers refused to cross into Canada, so American forces turned around without really fighting the British.

The Battle of Queenston Heights marked the second time Americans tried to invade Canada and failed.

19

In spite of these defeats on land, the Americans did meet some success at sea. One of the most famous battles took place off the coast of Massachusetts between the American ship *Constitution* and the British ship *Guerriere* in August 1812.

Cannonballs seemed to bounce right off the sides of the *Constitution,* which prompted one sailor to shout, "Huzza! Her sides are made of iron!" Actually, they were made of wood and covered with a thin sheet of copper. Nevertheless, the sailor's comments soon led to the *Constitution*'s nickname, Old Ironsides. The American ship, an example of great shipbuilding, defeated the *Guerriere* and secured its place in U.S. history.

American ships won a number of other sea battles. While these victories helped keep the Americans' spirits up, they didn't do much to change the course of the war. Slowly, the British were surrounding the U.S. coastline. Before long, they

20

The American ship Constitution *(left) earned its nickname Old Ironsides after defeating the British ship* Guerriere *in August 1812.*

formed a blockade of U.S. ports, stopping all U.S. trade. As with the embargo of 1807, businesses suffered, and the government went deeper into debt.

21

BATTLES OF 1813

In 1813, American troops invaded Canada again. In January, a battle at Raisin River ended in defeat for the Americans. Then in April, the Americans captured York (now Toronto) and held the capital of Upper Canada for a short time.

A major success for the Americans came in September during the most important sea battle of the war. U.S. soldiers

An American soldier's wife joins in battle.

22

During the Battle of Lake Erie, Oliver Hazard Perry's flagship was severely damaged. He and a small group of soldiers rowed through heavy gunfire to another ship in his fleet, from which he won the battle.

took control of Detroit after Oliver Hazard Perry led American ships in defeating the British on Lake Erie. It was then that Perry sent a famous message to his commander: "We have met the enemy and they are ours."

23

The Indian leader Tecumseh was killed at the Battle of the Thames, crushing Indian efforts to resist American settlers moving west.

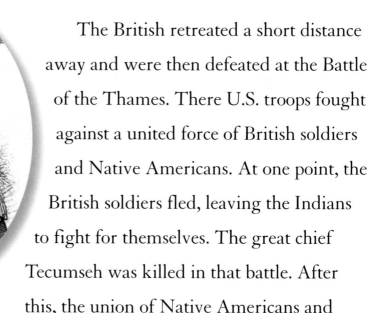

Tecumseh

The British retreated a short distance away and were then defeated at the Battle of the Thames. There U.S. troops fought against a united force of British soldiers and Native Americans. At one point, the British soldiers fled, leaving the Indians to fight for themselves. The great chief Tecumseh was killed in that battle. After this, the union of Native Americans and British against the American forces came to an end. Soon even more Indian land was taken away.

As the war continued, the United States suffered. In November, Americans were defeated by a small group of British forces at the Battle of Chrysler's Farm, about 100 miles (160 kilometers) from Montreal. By December, the British had crossed into northern New York. They burned Buffalo and the surrounding towns.

At home, the American citizens had their own struggles. New England, which relied on trade with other countries, was unable to do business. Merchants could not sell their goods, and they quickly lost money. Also, while fathers and brothers fought in the war, many families struggled to tend shops and run farms without them.

As James Madison began his second term as president, he assured the American people that "the war was just [fair] in its origin and necessary and noble in its objects." Whether or not the Americans liked being at war, he felt the nation had no choice in fighting against Great Britain.

25

BRITISH INVASION OF 1814

In 1814, the situation for the American forces grew much worse. The British had finally defeated the French, so they were free to concentrate all their efforts on the war in the United States. They doubled the number of troops fighting the Americans.

The British planned to invade at three key places in the United States. One force would enter from the north at Lake Champlain and sail down the Hudson River in New York. Capturing this area would block off access to New England. Another British force would come up from the south in New Orleans, Louisiana, where they could gain control of the Mississippi River. They would also attack from the middle of the country at Chesapeake Bay near Virginia and Washington, D.C.

The invasion at Chesapeake Bay was only supposed to distract the Americans away from more important battles in Lake Champlain and New Orleans.

26

However, it went so easily for the British that they continued on to Bladensburg (near Washington, D.C.) and defeated the Americans.

Then the British marched into Washington, the capital city. Under the leadership of Major General Robert Ross, the British troops set fire to the Capitol, which is the building where Congress meets. Burning

The British burn Washington, D.C.

27

British troops attack the President's House.

the building proved difficult since it was made of very
strong stone. The troops piled up books and curtains
and set them on fire. Then they headed toward the
President's House.

28

President Madison was not home as the troops advanced, but his wife, Dolley, was. She is credited for thinking quickly. Before she escaped, she took important papers and other valuable items. She also had a famous portrait of George Washington torn from the wall, packed up, and moved to safety. She got out just before the British arrived.

Dolley Madison saved important government papers from being destroyed during the attack on the President's House.

According to one story, the troops ate the dinner she had prepared for friends and then set fire to the house. Afterward, the British continued through the city, burning the Treasury Building and the Library of Congress.

29

BATTLE OF FORT MCHENRY

Next, the troops headed to Baltimore. The British were eager to invade that Maryland city because many fine American ships were built there. Destroying Baltimore would be a way to get back at the Americans for defeating British ships, which were a great source of pride to their country. The United States was worried.

Losing its shipbuilding companies wouldn't just be a blow to the war. It could hurt future trade, even after the war was over.

As the British troops approached Baltimore, the city prepared for battle. Major General Samuel Smith, a Revolutionary War hero, was leading the effort. He enlisted the help of all the citizens—

Samuel Smith

30

black, white, rich, and poor. Together, they dug trenches and put cannons in position. Major Smith also convinced the ship owners to sink their ships in the harbor. This would be a tricky way to block the British ships from entering the Baltimore port. The British would not be able to see the ships in the water and would get stuck trying to sail past them.

Guarding the Baltimore harbor was Fort McHenry. Flying above this five-sided fort was a huge American flag. There was no way the British ships could miss it as they sailed toward the city. The huge flag was meant to show the British that the Americans were not afraid of them.

The day the British arrived, there was another ship in the harbor. It was an American truce ship, which was a special ship used for talks with the British. Onboard was Francis Scott Key, an American lawyer who had been sent to arrange for the freedom of a prisoner of war. Key was successful in getting the man released, but he had to stay on the truce ship while the battle was fought.

31

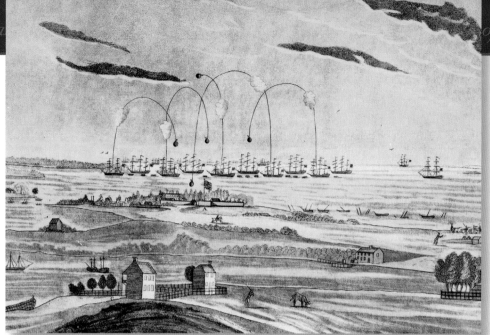

The British bomb Fort McHenry.

In the meantime, Sir George Cockburn, a British admiral, was discouraged by the sunken ships in the Baltimore harbor. He saw that he could not enter the harbor directly. He and his men would have to take Fort McHenry.

British ships began firing cannons at the fort while British soldiers landed nearby. The soldiers were to plan an attack while the cannon fire protected them. However, as the American troops returned fire, British commander General Robert Ross was killed. Without his leadership, the soldiers were confused. They received incorrect information and turned back.

32

For the next 25 hours, the British ships continued to fire on the fort, and the American soldiers fought back. All the while, Francis Scott Key watched the battle from his ship. The bright lights and deafening sounds of the battle were overwhelming. They stirred up strong patriotic feelings in Key. When the fighting finally stopped and he

Francis Scott Key watches the bombing of Fort McHenry from his truce ship.

saw the huge American flag still waving above the fort, he knew the British had been defeated. That battle inspired him to write a poem called "The Defense of Fort McHenry."

33

During the battle at Fort McHenry, Francis Scott Key wrote this poem that would later become the words to "The Star-Spangled Banner."

The end of the first verse is now well known to most Americans. Those lines read: "And the rockets' red glare, the bombs bursting in air/Gave proof through the night that our flag was still there./O say, does that star-spangled banner yet wave/O'er the land of the free and the home of the brave?"

As word of the victory spread, more and more people read Key's poem. Soon they were singing the words instead of just saying them. They sang the words to a tune that had been written by English composer John Stafford Smith in 1775. The words and the music soon became "The Star-Spangled Banner." In 1931, "The Star-Spangled Banner" officially became the American national anthem.

THE END OF THE WAR

The victory at Fort McHenry marked a major change in the War of 1812. A few weeks later, British troops entered the United States at Lake Champlain, expecting to easily defeat the Americans and head to New York City. Instead, U.S. troops pushed the British back into Canada.

As the war continued, both sides wished it would come to an end. The people of England were tired of paying taxes to support the expensive war, and the Americans worried about what would become of their new nation if they lost. So both sides began to talk about reaching an agreement.

Heading up the U.S. group seeking peace was John Quincy Adams, Henry Clay, and Albert Gallatin. The two sides met at Ghent, Belgium, and after five months of discussions, they signed a treaty on December 24, 1814. The treaty put an end to the fighting. However, it did not address the practice of impressment. Nor did it secure American rights at sea. It also stated that the British had

In December 1814, the Americans and the British signed the Treaty of Ghent, putting an end to the war.

to give back the land they had captured in the United States, and the Americans had to give back the land they had captured in Canada.

In other words, none of the problems that had caused the war were addressed in the treaty. Instead, everything just returned to the way it was before the war started. Even more amazing, both sides claimed to have won.

Evening Gazette Office,

Boston, Monday, 10, A.M.

The following most highly important handbill has just been issued from the Centinel press. We deem a duty that we owe our Friends and the Public to assist in the prompt spread of the Glorious News.

Treaty of PEACE signed and arrived.

Centinel Office, Feb. 13, 1815, 8 o'clock in the morning.

WE have this instant received in Thirty-two hours from New-York the following

Great and Happy News!
FOR THE PUBLIC.

To Benjamin Russell, Esq. Centinel-Office, Boston.
New-York, Feb. 11, 1815—Saturday Evening, 10 o'clock.

SIR—

I HASTEN to acquaint you, for the information of the Public, of the arrival here this afternoon of H. Br. M. sloop of war Favorite, in which has come passenger Mr. Carroll, American Messenger, having in his possession

A Treaty of Peace

Between this Country and Great-Britain, signed on the 26th December last.

Mr. Baker also is on board, as Agent for the British Government, the same who was formerly Charge des Affairs here.

Mr. Carroll reached town at eight o'clock this evening. He shewed to a friend of mine, who is acquainted with him, the pacquet containing the Treaty, and a London newspaper of the last date of December, announcing the signing of the Treaty.

It depends, however, as my friend observed, upon the act of the President to suspend hostilities on this side.

The gentleman left London the 2d Jan. The Transit had sailed previously from a port on the Continent.

This city is in a perfect uproar of joy, shouts, illuminations, &c. &c.

I have undertaken to send you this by Express—the rider engaging to deliver it by Eight o'clock on Monday morning. The expense will be 225 dollars:—If you can collect so much to indemnify me I will thank you to do so.

I am with respect, Sir, your obedient servant,
JONATHAN GOODHUE.

We most heartily felicitate our Country on this auspicious news, which may be relied on as wholly authentic.—Centinel.

This American announcement calls the Treaty of Ghent and the end of the war "great and happy news!"

Both England and the United States welcomed the peace treaty. Remember, though, that in 1814 people didn't have telephones, faxes, or e-mail. Communication happened by messengers or letters carried by ships, so news spread slowly. News of the Treaty of Ghent didn't reach the United States until February 11, 1815.

Not knowing that the war was already over, British troops started landing in New Orleans in late December 1814. On January 8, 1815, they fought American troops

Andrew Jackson led U.S. troops to victory at the Battle of New Orleans in January 1815. Jackson and his men hadn't yet heard that the war was over.

led by Major General Andrew Jackson. The Americans lost 13 men that day, and 60 were wounded. About 1,500 British were killed or wounded. It was a huge, unnecessary loss of life.

39

Andrew Jackson parades through New Orleans after his victory in battle.

The Battle of New Orleans may not have had an effect on the war, but it saved the city of New Orleans from being destroyed. It made Andrew Jackson an American hero, and he went on to become president of the United States.

As we look back at the War of 1812, it's easy to wonder why it was fought in the first place. Most of the causes of the war took care of themselves in the coming years. The British stopped trade blockades, and they stopped impressment. After the death of Chief Tecumseh, the United States quickly grew across the West.

Nevertheless, the War of 1812—a war the Americans tried to avoid—became a source of pride for the country. Patriotism increased, and the country grew more united. For the second time in 30 years, the Americans had stood up to the mighty British. This earned the United States more respect from countries throughout the world.

GLOSSARY

anthem—a song that serves as a symbol of a nation

blockade—a way of fighting a war by not allowing enemy troops or supplies to enter or leave an area

deserted—quit military service without permission

embargo—an official order that stops something from happening, such as the buying and selling of goods

impressment—the practice of forcing people into service against their will

invasion—a military attack that involves going into the enemy's country

privateer—an armed ship owned by a private citizen, not by the navy; privateers were hired out for use in wars

treaty—a formal agreement involving two or more countries

truce ship—a ship that carries people who try to make peace in a war or work to free prisoners; not a military ship

42

Did You Know?

- Napoleon Bonaparte became the leader of France after the French Revolution of 1789–1799. This is when the French people overturned the system of kings that had been ruling their country for centuries. Many historians think that the French were inspired by the success of the American Revolution just a few years earlier.

- Even today, the U.S. flag always flies over Fort McHenry, day and night, no matter the weather.

- Once the War of 1812 was over, the President's House was painted white to cover the marks left by the fire. It has officially been called the White House since 1901.

- In 1814, some leaders in New England were so fed up with the war they decided to take action. They held a meeting, called the Hartford Convention, in Connecticut. Some of the leaders pushed for New England to make peace with Great Britain on its own, even if the rest of the country didn't agree. These extremists came up with a plan for New England to form its own country, but the plan was rejected.

IMPORTANT DATES

Timeline

1807
In June, the British ship *Leopard* fires on the American ship *Chesapeake,* almost starting a war between the two countries.

1812
In June, Congress declares war on Great Britain; British forces capture Detroit in August.

1813
Under Oliver Hazard Perry, U.S. forces defeat the British fleet at Lake Erie; Tecumseh is killed at the Battle of the Thames.

1814
The British burn Washington, D.C.; Fort McHenry is attacked, and Francis Scott Key writes the poem that later becomes "The Star-Spangled Banner"; Treaty of Ghent ends the war in December.

1815
In January, Andrew Jackson leads the U.S. victory at the Battle of New Orleans.

IMPORTANT PEOPLE

ANDREW JACKSON (1767–1845)
War of 1812 military hero who went on to become the seventh president of the United States

FRANCIS SCOTT KEY (1779–1843)
American lawyer who wrote the poem that later became the words for "The Star-Spangled Banner"

DOLLEY MADISON (1768–1849)
First lady who is credited with saving valuable material from the President's House before it was burned during the War of 1812

JAMES MADISON (1751–1836)
Fourth president of the United States; was in office during the War of 1812

OLIVER HAZARD PERRY (1785–1819)
American naval commander who led the victory against the British at the Battle of Lake Erie

TECUMSEH (ca. 1768–1813)
Native American leader who allied with the British to defend Indian lands during the War of 1812

WANT TO KNOW MORE?

At the Library

Bartoletti, Susan Campbell. *The Flag Maker.* Boston: Houghton Mifflin, 2004.

Crewe, Sabrina. *The Writing of "The Star Spangled Banner."* Milwaukee, Wis.: Gareth Stevens, 2004.

Santella, Andrew. *James Madison.* Minneapolis: Compass Point Books, 2003.

Smolinski, Diane, and Henry Smolinski. *Battles of the War of 1812.* Chicago: Heinemann Library, 2003.

On the Web

For more information on the *War of 1812,* use FactHound to track down Web sites related to this book.

1. Go to *www.facthound.com*

2. Type in a search word related to this book or this book ID: 0756508487.

3. Click on the *Fetch It* button.

Your trusty FactHound will fetch the best Web sites for you!

46

On the Road

Erie Maritime Museum

150 E. Front St.

Erie, PA 16507

814/452-2744

To see the reconstructed *Niagara,*
one of the ships used in the
Battle of Lake Erie

Fort McHenry

End of East Fort Avenue

Baltimore, MD 21230-5393

410/962-4290

To visit the site of the famous battle

Look for more We the People books about this era:

The Alamo

The Arapaho and Their History

The Battle of the Little Bighorn

The Buffalo Soldiers

The California Gold Rush

The Chumash and Their History

The Creek and Their History

The Erie Canal

Great Women of the Old West

The Lewis and Clark Expedition

The Louisiana Purchase

The Mexican War

The Ojibwe and Their History

The Oregon Trail

The Pony Express

The Santa Fe Trail

The Transcontinental Railroad

The Trail of Tears

The Wampanoag and Their History

A complete list of We the People titles is available on our Web site:
www.compasspointbooks.com

47

INDEX

About the Author

Lucia Raatma received her bachelor's degree in English literature from the University of South Carolina and her master's degree in cinema studies from New York University. She has written a wide range of books for young people. When she is not researching or writing, she enjoys going to movies, practicing yoga, and spending time with her family. She lives in New York.

48